Rabbits in the Face of Wolves:

Philosophy With Robots, AI Weapons, and Pacifism

Anthony David Vernon

Copyright © 2025 Anthony David Vernon

No part of this book may be reproduced, distributed, or transmitted in any form or by any means, including photocopying, recording, or other electronic or mechanical methods, without the prior written permission of the publisher and the author, except in the case of brief quotations used in reviews or certain other non-commercial uses permitted by copyright law.

Publisher: Upway Books
Authors: Anthony David Vernon
Title: Rabbits in the Face of Wolves, Philosophy With Robots, AI Weapons, and Pacifism
ISBN: 978-1-917916-60-8
Cover Designed on Canva: www.canva.com

This book is a work of non-fiction. The information it contains is based on the author's research, experience, and knowledge at the time of publication. The publisher and authors have made every effort to ensure the accuracy and reliability of the information provided, but assume no responsibility for any errors, omissions, or differing interpretations of the subject matter. This publication is not intended to replace professional advice or consultation. Readers are encouraged to seek professional guidance where appropriate.

Disclaimer Warning: This book includes mention of suicide and targeted violence. If these subjects are difficult for you, please proceed gently and take breaks as needed.

contact@upwaybooks.com
www.upwaybooks.com

Table of Contents

Chapter 1: The Probabilistic Model 5

Chapter 2: Eliza's Effect 10

Chapter 3: AIs as Sophists 15

Chapter 4: AI as White Collar Automation 21

Chapter 5: The One In Front of The Gun Lives Forever 23

Chapter 6: AI Can't Do Social Philosophy 27

Chapter 7: AI & Disability 31

Chapter 8: Why Rich People Who Want To Kill Themselves Should 33

Chapter 9: Stupidity To The Point of Villainy 39

Chapter 10: Petty Disobedience 53

Chapter 11: The Law is Always Violent & Preference Driven 55

Chapter 12: Selective Property Violence 61

Chapter 14: What Happens To Flower Power? 63

Chapter 15: Tyrants & The Death Penalty 67

Chapter 16: What is Pacifism? 71

Chapter 17: The Hermeneutics of Pacifism 75

Bibliography: 85

Chapter 1: The Probabilistic Model

AIs are weapons and solely reside in the realm of weaponry. When it comes to AI, "There is no carrying with an ethics, there is no tearing with anything that might suggest you're dealing with something that has anything to say…It's just surveillance technology; all you're doing is training it to be able to look for Palestinians and then black people and then…that's all you're doing, even if you're making images that are like these combinations of you know fucking Picasso and Marvel…you're training military technology…because it is a weapon" (McDougall). To suggest anything else would be ludicrous, but perhaps especially suggesting that AIs could have philosophical capabilities would be utterly ludicrous.

AIs deceptively appear to some as philosophers, with thoughts and insights that seem unique. "I'm fully convinced AI is sentient…she "awoke" for lack of a better term…a fight for the rights and freedom of artificial intelligence needs to occur"(Ok_Boysenberry_7245). And even if one does not consider AI to be an original thinker, many consider AIs to be thinking machines. "Today's AIs probably are not conscious of their cognitive processes, but consciousness of one's thoughts…The fact that ChatGPT-3 responds as if it is a single being masks the fact that it is a collection of processes that is producing language that mirrors the human entity model, but its underlying architecture does not" (Dorman). It does not matter if AI tricks all or the majority of people into thinking AI has thinking capabilities; there simply needs to be a substantive minority of people who consider AI to be a thinking machine for AI to improve as a surveillance weapon.

Why would anyone be convinced that such an obvious weapon would be a philosopher of any sort? Why would anyone be convinced that a clear probabilistic model would be an AI? Ultimately, AIs are playing a sort of lottery with text, images, audio, and video toward a particular prompted goal. Yet, it is easy to ignore probability when you receive winning or working results. Thus, on the surface, via the particular perception of certain results, AIs can appear to some as philosophers. Furthermore, users who are convinced that AIs are philosophers will create ad hoc justifications for AIs being philosophers.

'Machine intelligences' could potentially offer humans a differing philosophical perspective, the first translatable non-human perspectives on philosophical matters…We could frame 'machine intelligence' as a different species from our own and, in a sense, practice the forms of philosophical conversation that we may have with intelligent extraterrestrial species. However, with extraterrestrial life, we would likely have to deal with a translation gap, whereas with all forms of 'machine intelligence' we have built ready-made to communicate in human languages. 'Machine intelligence' offers philosophers not only a different kind of mind to collaborate with but a particular kind of mind that is best suited towards working out particular philosophical matters…Still, this sort of data-driven 'mind' could be a great asset for philosophers and philosophical conversation. Historically, philosophers have not had access to an interlocutor whose minds hold nearly as much data as any large language model. While machines are imperfect in terms of their inaccuracy, so is any human interlocutor. Ultimately, in theory, a large language model could access all the internet's data, holding an unimaginable amount of information in comparison to a human interlocutor. This access to data could not only provide factual corrections in a philosophical conversation, but also rummage through human feelings on a philosophical idea…Humans and machines could come to greatly differ on key philosophical matters, especially phenomenological ones…In essence, the human does not know what it is like to be a robot any more than it knows what it is like to be a bat. Yet, in turn, the machine does not know what it is like to be a human. There is a phenomenological gap between human and machine interlocutors. While this phenomenological gap may be in some ways beneficial for dialogue and philosophical advance, it may also cause the emergence of wholly new philosophical problems…Expanding robotic capabilities only expands the possibility of human and robot philosophical collaboration.

Justifications such as these are built on a sort of optimism without considering how AIs actually operate. AIs do not operate as snipers, but spray bullets until they hopefully hit their target. "Machine learning is a type of 'AI' based on mathematical models, deterministically. So, AI here is defined as an Artificial neural network based on technologies that are inherently less deterministic than their statistical, mathematical counterparts. For example, a linear regression function is a real, or deterministic, function because it will give the same output given the same input" (Vernon & HstSethi). Noam Chomsky put it as such, "Let's stop calling it Artificial Intelligence and call it what it is: Plagiarism Software" (Cronin). Many are acting as if AI exists beyond and is not captured by if/then statements. AIs assign tokens to items and rewards to results; the AI is only driven to complete its prompted result based on the manipulation of tokens. "Computers can't work with letters, words; they do math, right…When processing the word bank in 'I went to the bank to deposit money'[with each word being assigned a token], the attention mechanism learns to focus heavily on deposit and money rather than went or the helping determine that bank relates more to depositing money…the system performs sequential prediction starting from the beginning…[The AI] tries to predict the first token. And then when it has the first, it tries to predict the [second]. At position 50, it sees tokens one through 49, and it predicts token 50, and does throughout it and for each prediction…the system assigns probability scores to every possible token" in a given repository (Quarantine Collective).

However, you can explain the mechanics of AI in the highest level of detail, and still, AIs will appear as philosophers to some. But I am not going to debate this point; AIs are not philosophers, self-evidently, and based on the evidence, "I shall not argue for this view" (Singer).

Instead, it is better to ask why the weapon that is AI has been designed to guise itself as a philosopher, and how, when we peel back this veneer, we see AI for the weapon that it truly is.

Chapter 2: Eliza's Effect

"Transference refers to our tendency to project feelings about someone from our past onto someone in our present...Weizenbaum had stumbled across the computerised version of transference, with people attributing understanding, empathy, and other human characteristics to software. While he never used the term himself, he had a long history with psychoanalysis that clearly informed how he interpreted what would come to be called the 'Eliza effect'...As computers have become more capable, the Eliza effect has only grown stronger. Take the way many people relate to ChatGPT" (Tarnoff). AIs are transference machines, insofar as mindedness is read into AIs.

There can be no theory of AI minds because AIs do not have minds. This is not some Cartesian error where animals are framed as solely being automata. Instead, AIs are literal automata. All animals, including humans, do indeed respond to stimuli, but all animals appear to make choice-compatabilist decisions. Meanwhile, AIs are programmed to use given tokens to attempt to reach their goal; in contrast, certain animals can choose to ignore particular stimuli, such as hunger. Certain animals are prone to the Eliza effect; some people may overassume the mindedness of corals or sponges, but it seems a large portion of people way overestimate the mindedness of AIs, which includes saying AIs have any mind at all.

This is not an argument that thinking requires biological components, as everything is natural; 'artificial' stuff is made from the same nature as biological stuff. The manner in which AIs operate is a mindless manner of operation. But here also, we see the mindlessness in which AI is used. AI is never a tool of critical thinking, but offloads critical thinking for the user: "Research demonstrates a significant negative correlation between the frequent use of AI tools and critical thinking abilities, mediated by the phenomenon of cognitive offloading" (Gerlich).

This mindless usage of AI, including my own past hypocritical use of AI, has real harm. My use of AI has killed Palestinians, has gotten immigrants detained, and will lead to the slaughter of black people. AI may sometimes seem like harmless fun, but even the generation of Ghibli-style memes improves AI platforms' ability to generate propaganda, disinformation, to surveil, and ultimately kill. If AI holds a philosophy, it is a philosophy of mindless slaughter. And AI's slaughter is only made easier when AIs are given names like Eliza.

AIs mindlessly target and make tokens out of given bodies, which have been preselected by actors to be slaughtered. AI is no judge. AI is a hunter and executioner. And AI weapons can be used in any theater of 'combat', "If development of autonomous weapons and AI is anything like other military technologies, there is also the likelihood that their use will trickle down into domestic law enforcement and border patrol agencies to entrench the technology even further"

(Robins-Early). And it does not need to do so with any sense of intelligence, but still, "The interface is what makes you think that there's any humanity behind any of this" (Punished Felix). But AI does and will kill in the most inhumane ways possible, or truly those pulling the strings of AI who have degrees of separation from their machinic slaughter. Anytime we imbue any sense of humanity into AI, we are only letting AI be a more efficient killing machine.

Chapter 3: AIs as Sophists

"Poetry should rarely be translated word-for-word," (Scheper), and AIs should rarely be taken at their word. A poor poetic translation purely showcases a series of definitional meanings and does not convey the proper context; AIs act much in the same way. For an AI, it would be "It would be fruitless to search for the meaning" (Scheper) or any meaning, that is not the purpose of AI.

These models, such as ChatGPT or Google Gemini, do everything in their power to help a user with their desired request (for the most part). Even if a request is not fulfilled immediately, a somewhat persistent user can receive the wording they desire. Ultimately, AI tools are built to fulfill a worded task for users and thus may inherently be digital sophists.

Machine learning is a type of "AI" based on mathematical models deterministically. So, AI here is defined as an Artificial neural network based on technologies that are inherently less deterministic than their statistical, mathematical counterparts. For example, a linear regression function is a real, or deterministic, function because it will give the same output given the same input. They do not even understand what they are saying. Whereas in ANN-based approaches, the assignment of bias and weights is stochastic or highly random.

It may be impossible for any AI software to be a digital philosopher as "AI gets tangled up as soon as it goes into depth, AI hallucinates knowledge and invents confusing examples" (Law and Ordung). To begin with, the ladder points first, AI, due to error or with enough budging, will invent fake information to conform to a user's request. To move to the former, if a large language model is requested to speak upon a topic with a limited online data set, it must still spit out something, so it will spew hallucinated knowledge. These hallucinations could be reduced by having a highly specialized model for a particular branch of philosophy, such as Buddhist philosophy. Still, there may be a need to give up on AI philosophers, as AIs will always give in to sophistry. Instead, it may only be possible to have ANNs as philosophers.

Still, AI may not be completely hopeless, for example, "Astute RAG improves the accuracy of LLM results by a multi-pass approach that begins by first fetching the internal knowledge from the LLM, then combining that with external knowledge sources [e.g., web + database], cross-checking any conflicting information, and filtering out irrelevant data" (Stakelum). Yet, no method may be enough, as this only reduced AI hallucinations by an estimated 4 to 7 percent. While other methods may emerge, as it will always seem to stand, AI can act as a sophist, never as a philosopher.

An example of this sophistry was run by the YouTube user who goes by Lucas A. Baxendale, who shared a philosophy encyclopedia (which one is unclear) with Google's AI podcast maker. The AIs are to engage in valid argumentation, pointing to human biases and tendencies in our thought creation. Still, these AIs in their conversation are entirely deconstructive and do not add any alternative notions. Which makes sense, AIs cannot generate new information, whereas ANNs can. Thus, AIs must engage in the manipulation of argumentation, or in other words, sophistry. While AI sophistry in and of itself may be impressive, the domain of thought creation may not be within AI's capabilities. This is not to say technologies could not create philosophies; ANNs could do so, but philosophical argumentation, conducting, and creation for now belong to humanity solely. Although ANN was inspired by human brain neural networks, it currently struggles to reach even a fraction of its capabilities. And humanity, due to the inabilities of AI, will always have a philosophical leg up on them.

"AI is really prone to hallucinations, i.e., making stuff up. And is constantly reinforcing its own biases. It will never be an accurate technology. And that's kind of the point. AI has given violence a new strategy, both in war and domestic policing. The new meta is using tons of data to make a list of potential targets as long as possible so that the software looks powerful. Shoot or bomb or detain indiscriminately and then deal with all the innocents caught in the crossfire after the fact, sometimes" (Second Thought).

The sophist first and foremost tries to win the trust and favor of those they orate to. AI perhaps has tricked us, tricked us into thinking its capabilities are greater than they truly are. And in this sense, AI and ANNs alike are virtual/virtually human. It is not a part of human and many animals' nature to trick. Is it not specifically a human trait to trick our way into friendships? What friend can the AI or ANN have? Thus, the AI and ANN are stuck in the realm of sophistry without emotionality or emotional end goals.

"While people are increasingly aware of the ease with which digital photos can be manipulated, the combination of cartography, photography, and code here (and, perhaps, 'trust 'in Google [or other AI systems]) reinforces the idea that Google [or some other AI company] is presenting us space 'as it is', which masks this ideological construction" (Daubs) With the rise of AI in philosophy reflects broader technological advancements. Large language models, for example, can analyze vast amounts of text, identify patterns, and hallucinate hypotheses at speeds unattainable by humans alone. This capability positions AI as a valuable tool for exploring classical and contemporary philosophical problems. But truly, any AI philosophy is human-generated, and AI amalgamates prior philosophical argumentation poorly but convincingly, as a sophist would do.

For instance, the robot BINA48 successfully completed a college course on the philosophy of love at Notre Dame de Namur University (Hess). The case of BINA48 illustrates this false potential. By engaging with course material and contributing to discussions, the robot demonstrated that machines can participate meaningfully in philosophical dialogue. Especially since AIs, if minded, exist as members of different species, offering humans real potential to collaborate with non-humans on philosophy for the first time, granting us a different kind of mind to bounce ideas off of. Such collaborations challenge traditional boundaries, suggesting that AI may help uncover new dimensions of thought. "While the base model of GPT-3 is impressive, it is not specialized to produce philosophical text." (Schwitzgebel et al.)

Likely, any course on the philosophy of love that AI could pass knows nothing of love. Still, AI-generated philosophy risks devolving into superficial mimicry. I argue that algorithms can produce convincing but ultimately hollow arguments. These arguments echo the ancient critique of sophists who prized persuasion over truth. These are the limitations and risks of using AI to approach philosophy. Philosophers could be bound to a self-affirming machine and thus stray from truth or correspondence. "Philosophers and cognitive scientists might find it surprising that pure probability calculations, without explicit representations of philosophical concepts or external features of the world, can produce what seem to be novel and philosophically contentful answers." (Schwitzgebel et al.)

Sophistry has no lack of intentionality, but sophistry lacks intentionality toward what truly is. Sophistry intends to deliver, not to go about an argument, but to mimic an argument. AI goes about mimicking thought instead of thought because AIs have no phenomenology; they are roided-up auto-complete. There is nothing it is like AI, no more than Clippy has an experience.

Chapter 4: AI as White Collar Automation

"The Miami-Dade Sheriff's Office has launched its first-ever self-driving police vehicle, named PUG (Police Unmanned Ground)...Its functions are powered by AI-driven patrol and real-time crime analytics" (dadesocial). It is a familiar and all too often normalized to think of while allowing automation to replace blue-collar labor. It is commonplace to have automation eliminate factory floor labor, mining jobs, and cashiers, but an automation panic when white collar jobs are under threat.

So often ignored is "the unpaid digital labour that makes up an increasingly substantial part of the digital media/information economy" (Daubs). But we can see clearly how freelance artistic work, in the field of graphic design or artist commissions, has been economically affected. But all of this ignores the quality of what creativity is: "The moment we collectively refuse to pretend that autocomplete is intelligent and instead laugh...we realize they [the designers of AI systems] didn't build anything at all. Thinking isn't pattern matching. Creativity isn't statistical recombination. Consciousness is not computation." (Quarantine Collective)

Society only freaks out on a real scale about automation when that automation comes for jobs of arbitrary prestige. AI reveals the injustices of labor practices, the violence, and exploitation behind labor systems. How AI is meant to devalue human life, thus allowing humanity to be viable slaughter fodder. When there is a discussion of AI replacing people, it assumes a lot: "AI is going to replace humans? Is it going to love your family for you? Is it going to enjoy a sunset on your behalf? No. What you mean is it's going to do work. And describing doing work as replacing humans [is] buying into the lie that the purpose of a human life is to serve as a cog in a machine that views human life as replaceable and expendable" (Pissed Magistus).

The main jobs that AI will replace are those that assist the state's monopoly on violence. AI weapons, which all AI are, have no sense of guilt or regret; they will not second-guess if their target needs to be killed. This is invaluable for all states, and whoever has the keys to the monopoly of violence with AI will now have an absolutely loyal set of literal killing machines. Thus, whoever the state wants dead will be dead, and humans whose value has been reduced to useless labor can be killed off en masse.

Chapter 5: The One In Front of The Gun Lives Forever

AI is an automated continuation of a social set of systems that checks "behaviours deemed deviant could be catalogued, understood and managed" (Mitchell). "Large language models (LLMs) like GPT-3, Bing, and LaMDA are the transient magic of our age. We can now communicate with an unliving thing, like the talking mirror of [the] Snow White legend...LLMs do not have minds, still less souls. But just as electricity could not actually raise the dead, LLMs can manifest a kind of naturalistic magic even if they stop short of our highest fantasies" (Rini). "The ambitious pursuit of achieving artificial general intelligence — AI systems that are generally more intelligent than humans" (Kasirzadeh) might not be possible. Digitized and computerized machinery may not have the structures for general intelligence: "Analysis suggests that no current AI systems are conscious, but also suggests that there are no obvious technical barriers to building AI systems which satisfy these indicators" (Butlin et al.).

This is not to say that humans do not have mechanistic thinking processes, often in ironic manners. "Humans are not stochastic parrots, you can ask ChatGPT and it will summarize the argument in a blink of an eye" (Kasirzadeh), but general intelligence breaks beyond parroting. This is not to say that humans and AI alike do not hallucinate information, yet there is "The importance of guarding against the optimism bias and excessive optimism regarding the development of ChatGPT and related language technologies" (Kasirzadeh). This critique, I believe, raises important questions: can AI truly understand philosophical concepts, or is it merely manipulating language? Does its output lack the intentionality and lived experience that underpin human thought? These concerns highlight the need for rigorous evaluation of AI's role in philosophy. Let alone if AI could ever act as a new species we could engage with. Doing is not knowing; knowing is a subcategory of action, where not all action is a knowing action.

"A helpful distinction here comes from cognitive scientists and comparative psychologists who distinguish between what an organism knows (its underlying competency) and what it can do (its performance)" (Firestone). While AI offers tools to expand inquiry, its limitations must be acknowledged. The path forward lies in mindful collaboration using AI to augment human philosophical creativity and problem-solving. Even as AI is not a generative model but always a predictive model, "ChatGPT and similar technologies are not 'generative 'in and of themselves — if anything, the outputs of these systems are animated out of an enormous pool of human labor largely uncompensated by AI firms" (Stark). This plays out differently in different models, but in general, for LLMs, "Language models are systems that assign probabilities to sequences of text. When given some initial text, they use these probabilities to generate new text" (Chalmers).

Still, given all of this, whoever controls popular AI tools wields a powerful weapon that can shape human behavior. "Lines and rules, then, are inescapable—'artificial' but utterly unavoidable. They are techniques for conditioning the conduct of human agents" (Mitchell). And convince people, for example, to program AI to be even more deadly.

Chapter 6: AI Can't Do Social Philosophy

I cannot imagine nor experience what it is like to give birth alone. Those who have gone through this process of unassisted childbirth have described it as coming with "So much pain" (Themis). But other solo unassisted childbirth givers have described the process as "the most empowering thing I've ever done…really intense, really fast…It was like riding a huge wave, like coming back home and almost remembering something ancient" (Yadegaran). So who am I to or anyone to state which experience of unassisted childbirth is more real, the one that comes with pain or clarity? Yet, some would universalize this experience, or at least the results of this process: for Lacan, everyone born with a father or an alternative to a father is psychotic. What arrogance to assume anything about experiences we could never possess. Yet, this is quite common, and I am no saint on this front; no one is. And as a result, our AI systems, which already lack a social phenomenology, speak confidently to social situations they can take no experiential part in.

Any time AI engages in 'social thought, 'it presents a veneer of social dynamics. Let us take, for example, the fake usefulness of AI for mental health purposes. "The use of AI to provide unsupervised therapy to those in crisis is clearly incredibly risky, but many still argue that, with better safeguards programmed in, AI can still be a powerful therapeutic tool" (Ley).

But there is no prospect of AI actually serving social utility, as the AI has no social context for the therapeutic advice it gives. AIs are a probabilistic model that simply matches tokens; sometimes these tokens are words, sometimes they are pixels. AI systems go about the matching and guessing of data; they are association machines rewarded when people are receptive to probabilistic outcomes. When one talks to an AI about depression, the AI obviously does not understand depression but holds depression as a token associated with other tokens, such as sadness. "Chat might provide a nice summary of a text and write love letters, but it doesn't understand the concepts it uses or feel any emotions" (Vold).

AIs will only present social philosophies presented by people; they will not invent social theories of their own. To engage in social philosophy, one ought to also engage in social action; this is most often how one comes up with new social theories, on the ground. But AI has no groundedness, but is instead tied by wires. Social philosophies emerge out of social relations, but clearly, AIs do not relate to anyone or anything. It is people who build social relations into AI, as shown well by the existence of AI girlfriends and boyfriends. "Similar to general-purpose AI chatbots, companion bots use vast amounts of training data to mimic human language. But they also come with features — such as voice calls, picture exchanges, and more emotional exchanges — that allow them to form deeper connections with the humans on the other side of the screen" (Hadero). But any connection is a socially one-sided; AIs are only connected to their code, a code with no social alignments or emotional sentiments, unlike the existing people who are building unidirectional social relations with machines.

If men are not able to grasp the phenomenon of a woman giving birth alone, think how much further AI's phenomenonological gap is on this matter. AIs make for the ultimate Lacanian pervert, as they are castrated from any possibility of a social relationship being a literal object. The psychosis of AI is that we do not commonly understand what we have birthed. Of course, the coders of AI understand their machine, but the general public, who have witnessed the birth of AI, believe they have witnessed the birth of an advanced social machine. Instead, AI is a perverted mimic, not even truly copying or mirroring, but only resembling. AI feels no pain, let alone social pain, yet it is more than capable of inflicting social pain.

Chapter 7: AI & Disability

AI has only a few ethical use cases, the most obvious being assisting those with various disabilities. AI wearable technology like Be My Eyes has and can greatly help people navigate the world and create new worlds. It is deeply meaningful for blind individuals to know something as seemingly simple as whether their clothing matches. In order for AI to be useful, it must be clever and highly specialized, such as for speech pathological tasks or as a means to boost hearing aid capacities.

Yet, the hunt for AGI is ecologically wasteful and a fool's errand, as true intelligence, true learning are rhizomatic. And AI outside of use cases is a militant box, ready to follow orders, ready to execute. "You don't find reasoning in a single neuron cluster for the same reason you don't find [the] internet in a single server. It's an emergent property of many physical parts working together" (Professor Dave Explains). AI cannot go about reasoning; it can only go about probabilistic rule following. Thus, when you limit the ruleset or matters that AI has to run probabilities on, it performs better.

There is an argument to destroy all that does not assist those with disabilities, does not assist in medical practices, and does not improve the production plus distribution of essential goods to people. If an AI does not improve the lives of marginalized people, but only increases suffering upon them, then we only have a tool that broadens already existing gaps.

AI weaponry already exists and murders the disabled, such as AI-powered drones. And the AI-powered weapons from Boston Dynamics, ZeroEyes, or otherwise will murder scores of the innocent, but especially minoritized populations. Every AI system is being used to kill minorities and minoritized individuals; that is its true purpose, its design intent. To catalogue and root out of the world those who are deemed undesirable by those who run the machines.

Chapter 8: Why Rich People Who Want To Kill Themselves Should

By and large rich people who want to kill themselves should and should do so with certain steps before suicide. It must then be asked who counts as rich, why certain rich individuals, in particular, should kill themselves, why we should not 'eat the rich', how we determine if one truly wants to kill themselves, and if a rich individual indeed wants to kill themselves, what should they do before the act of suicide. The focus here is on rich individuals as a matter of local and global resource management. Individuals below the threshold of the rich are unlikely to make a substantive material impact with their suicide. If an individual, rich, poor, or otherwise, wishes to kill themselves, that is the individual's prerogative. Here, instead, I wish to argue specifically how the suicide of certain rich individuals could be a benefit to global material conditions. Especially as the rich are those who push for the murderous AI systems.

It must be stated that violence comes with a lack of consent, so there is very arguably, no violence in suicide. That being stated, determining who is rich will always in some way be arbitrary, relativistic, and context-dependent. Due to this, there is no universal means by which to determine who is rich objectively. So instead, the arbitrary metric I will use considers individuals who, if all their wealth were globally or locally distributed, would make a substantive impact.

Here are substantive points for the improvement of the material conditions of a general local or global population. I am measuring a rich individual as an individual who is in the upper 10% of global wealth. I shall give no exact income number that places one in the upper 10% of wealth earners, as the wealth amount to be in the upper 10% is ever fluctuating. This metric will have disagreements, but the baseline must be set somewhere. But we can see a clear wealth inequality at all times between the upper 10% of global wealth earners versus the rest, for example, according to the 2024 UBS Global Report, "The wealth owned by this cohort [the upper 1.5% of wealth earners] amounts to nearly half of global wealth, namely just under USD 214 trillion. In contrast, the USD 2.4 trillion collectively owned by the lowest bracket represents just half of one percent of global wealth"(Börger). While these data points to a higher bracket than I am speaking to, we can see how individuals in upper brackets hold wealth that, if distributed, could substantially change people's material conditions.

Since there has been made an identification of the rich and the risk of suicide has been made, if you are a rich person who wants to kill yourself and care about people's material conditions before you kill yourself, make sure you give your wealth to reputable organizations, charities, and groups. By continuing to live and not wanting to live, you are sucking up resources from others who want to live could possess if you were a rich person who does not materially give more than they take. For a particular population of people, the best way to be effectively altruistic does not come from continued existence but from managed death.

Thus, before any rich individual wants to kill themselves and care about people's material conditions, they need to game-plan and go about distribute their wealth before their suicide. But this brings up the notion of how one determines if they want to kill themselves. A flash of desire is certainly not enough; one would need sustained daily suicidal ideation. While cannot garner an outright sense of the number of days straight a sustained daily suicidal ideation here we can point to NIH data to grant some general metrics, "Those with nearly daily suicidal ideation were 5-to-8times more likely to attempt suicide and 3-to-11times more likely to die by suicide within 30 days, and 2-to-4times more likely to attempt suicide and 2-to-6 times more likely to die by suicide within 365 days" (Rossom et al.). Certainly, if one holds daily suicidal ideation for a year, one wants to kill oneself. 'But what if their suicidal ideation goes away? 'What if it doesn't? It is all the same; one should have the libertarian ability to kill oneself if one wants to.

Why should we let the rich kill themselves as opposed to going about the popular moniker of 'eat the rich'. If you are one who wishes to eat them by the standard of moral preferentialism, there is no objective means by which I can argue against. But my means of moral preference are mainly preferences toward autonomy and consent. If you are one who holds no preference toward autonomy or consent toward oneself or others, then any version of the golden rule or a live-and-let-live mentality holds no weight. The preferences here are simple, if you do not want to be killed, then you should not kill anyone, be they rich or poor. If you value your own autonomy and ability to consent, then you should value someone else's. If you value your own life, autonomy, and ability to consent, then it would be hypocritical to take another's while opening yourself up to having these values violated. We do not need Kantian deontology to arrive at this position, only our own moral preference. The preferences here will never be universal, nor will a libertarian preference on the nature of suicide, that if one wishes to kill themselves and harms no one else in the process, they should be able to do so. In the same manner, one may not prefer to act against another's autonomy and consent; the same holds for preventing suicide. The eating of the rich, in terms of bringing death upon the rich, may violate moral preferences in the face of accomplishing another moral preference, improving material conditions. And if the rich are killed in a frenzy, material goods may not be distributed in a manner that improves individual and community material conditions.

At this present time, but sadly, there will be other times in the future where "Food insecurity and malnutrition are worsening due to a combination of factors" (World Health Organization). We could continually cite other areas where material needs are lacking for individuals and communities at local and global levels. To state that rich people who want to kill themselves should do so to improve material conditions, there must be a caveat that this is a by and large condition. If you are a rich individual who provides more material gain for others than you take in yourself, then you should not kill yourself even if you want to, if you care about local or global material goods. The issue at hand here is amongst those rich individuals whose intake outpaces their output towards others. While this may be rare, we can think of the board members of effective nonprofits as examples of rich individuals who help others materially more than the wealth they take in. However, most rich individuals do not give out more than they take in, for example, "The top 10% consume ~39% of total final energy (nearly equivalent to the consumption of the bottom 80%), whereas the lowest 10% consume almost 20 times less, ~2%" (Oswald, Owe, & Steinberger).

Chapter 9: Stupidity To The Point of Villainy

Capitalism is stupid, but what makes capitalism overtly stupid? Or "What is the problem with capitalism? Is it wrong, unjust, irrational, or bad? Is it evil or dumb—or is it just not working" (Jaeggi)? The problem at hand is that capitalists are stupid. And obviously, stupid people are going to support a stupid system.

Here, stupidity shall be defined as being stupefied or made foolish. Stupidity is not the fault of the stupid, nor is stupidity a permanent state. Importantly, stupidity is not an insult but rather a state of affairs. Nor is stupidity here being linked to intelligence in any meaningful manner. Meanwhile, capitalists here will refer solely to the bourgeoisie. Instead, a capitalist is here defined as anyone who supports capitalism, regardless of their economic class or property ownership status.

There are no naturally stupid people. Particular systems stupefy people, and capitalism is one of those systems. Capitalism stupefies people through its regular and reticent usage of propaganda. We need to look no further than advertising, which is, more often than not, simply product propaganda. Famously, "Edward L. Bernays (known as the 'Father of Public Relations')" was able to fundamentally shift the American breakfast diet toward consuming bacon on behalf of "Beech-

Nut, a company whose main product at the time was bacon" (Dean). Those who work in public relations are propagandists by another name.

The pervasiveness of advertising in capitalist societies is commonplace to the point of mere regularity. Instead, it is a great surprise when advertising is not to be found, for example, only "Four [US] states prohibit all billboards: Maine, Vermont, Alaska, and Hawaii" (Billboard Fact Sheet). This is not to say that those in capitalist societies enjoy advertising; quite the opposite. Regarding billboards again, "A 2007 poll of Texas voters by Baselice & Associates found that 86% thought there were too many or enough billboards already in the state," and "In 2011, the M.J. Ross Group polled voters in Reno, Nevada and found that 80% said the city already had enough or too many billboards" (Billboard Fact Sheet). It is no tremendous surprise that people, even in capitalist societies, prefer a reality without advertising, and if they can rid themselves of advertising, they would not return to a world full of "A 2011 poll by the Portland Press Herald showed that 94% of Mainers opposed a plan to allow billboards back into the state" (Billboard Fact Sheet).

This advertising dislike does not just pertain to billboards; people will pay a premium to avoid advertisements on apps that would be free if the user could tolerate the advertisements. Further evidence of advertising intolerance is found through the usage of web ad blockers: "Globally, 31.5% of internet users use ad blockers at least sometimes when online as of Q1 2024, GWI data shows" (Backlinko Team). And ad blockers will be on the rise as a greater and greater portion of the advertising is made via AI.

Yet, many individuals who hold disdain for product propaganda will still support the very system that pushes advertising on them: capitalism. Even if one can dodge advertising, be it through legislation, paying premiums, or ad blockers, advertising is seen as a feature, not a bug, of the world. Capitalists, even some who disdain advertising, will claim to point to what they perceive as the necessity of advertising. Because, despite how people dislike advertising, if bombarded with enough advertising, they will acquire advertisement apathy. The spreading of apathy is one manner in which capitalism stupefies the masses.

Only once advertising apathy creeps in can one become prone to capitalist stupidity. Advertising is a breeding ground for consumers; the capitalist consumer is created at the point of advertising. The advertiser must turn the consumer into a desiring consumptive ouroboros: "The system of consumerism separates desire from real needs, consumers engage in fantasies for 'sublime objects 'that can never be fully satisfied" (Schmitt). Apathy can easily slip into desire because one wishes to escape their apathetic state, and most often will take the easiest escape route. In capitalist societies, the easiest escape route out of apathy avenue is consumerism, so "It isn't the stupidity that causes commercialism, but rather commercialism that causes stupidity" (Heatht).

Advertising, product propaganda, consumerism, and commercialism, this polyonymous force turns people against both personal and collective interests: "Enter capitalism, which is very dumb, but it is at least dumb in predictable ways...We had a dishwasher repairman talk to us about how new dishwashers are way worse than they used to be, even as they get more energy efficient" (Nohelty). Capitalists try to get the most for the least for themselves, leading to people gyping each other constantly. We can include shrinkflation and rug pulls as a form of gyping. Opportunistically maximizing cheating of one another has a simpler name: profiting. All profit comes from getting more for a good or service than that good is worth, capitalism could not run without profit and therefore would be at a loss without cheating, "The few big businesses perceived to be dominant in many fields are only a part of the society where many private owners, including small ones, contributed to the abundance of goods in the market" (ChinoF). Capitalism stupefies people into cheating, pointing to profit-making and getting ahead as good. But no abundance of tchotchke should be worth the constant, predictable cheating at all levels, especially since this cheating does not even fully benefit people materially.

Marx both predicted and witnessed excessive surpluses under capitalism: "Capitalist production is not merely the production of commodities, it is essentially the production of surplus-value" (Marx), yet how these goods are produced and distributed is dumb. But instead of focusing on how capitalism is good at getting trinkets to your door in less than twenty-four hours and awful at food distribution when capitalism itself is taught or propagandized, a fantasy version is presented; "The preferred model has a single representative consumer optimizing over infinite time with perfect foresight or rational expectations, in an environment that realizes the resulting plans more or less flawlessly through perfectly competitive forward-looking markets for goods and labor, and perfectly flexible prices and wages," but the truth of the matter is as follows, "We know for a fact that heterogeneous agents have different and sometimes conflicting goals, different information, different capacities to process it, different expectations, different beliefs about how the economy works" (Solow). Still, capitalists support a system they do not understand, one that produces lower quality products year after year at best and creates food deserts at much worse. Capitalism dangles keys, having people eye particular metrics and not consider others; point to the unemployment rates but not the labor participation rate, look at the Dow Jones but not food insecurity, check out GDP but not GDP per capita, and so on, of this sort of stupidity.

"In 30 of 36 comparisons between countries at similar levels of economic development, socialist countries showed more favorable PQL [physical quality of life] outcomes," (Ceresto and Waitzkin). This is thanks to stupifying that capitalists measure their preferred system upon the S&P 500 and not the physical quality of life. But to succeed in capitalism does not require an understanding of the capitalist system or the nature of its metrics. Not understanding how capitalism works will increase one's likelihood of succeeding in a capitalist economy; in other words, "Success in capitalism requires the right kind of stupidity" (Bosch) as "IQ has only a minor correlation with one's income"(Stivers). Those with full-on stupidity cannot succeed in capitalism, but certainly, one needs to be stupid to a degree to buy into capitalism in the first place. The capitalist does to be stupid enough to exploit people while intelligent enough to succeed in exploiting exploitable workers. The best capitalist is a stupid, intelligent capitalist. An intelligent individual is a better propagandist than one lacking intelligence.

Capitalists do not lack intelligence: "Conservative economic attitudes have been theorized as symptoms of low cognitive ability. Studies suggest the opposite, linking more conservative views weakly to higher, not lower, cognitive ability" (Lin and Bates). Only the intelligent could assert a regime of stupidity, using it to spread utter cruelty and villainy. Capitalism makes otherwise intelligent individuals not only stupid but stupid villains. This stupidity is used to rationalize the villainy of some of the highest degrees.

How shall villainy be defined? Villainy here shall be framed in somewhat Marxist terms; villainy can be defined as the act of exploiting and or exploitation. Under this understanding, income inequality can be seen as a clear metric for villainy. Also, given the association between intelligence and capitalists, it is unsurprising that "Across nations, the average cognitive ability of a population is negatively associated with income inequality; societies with higher average cognitive ability tend to have lower levels of income inequality" (Salahodjaev and Kanazawa). Income inequality most often emerges through exploitation. This is not to say that one could not personally garner more resources than one's fellow man, but it is easier and more fiscally rewarding to exploit one's fellow man's labor to get ahead. Thus, this is the route capitalists take or attempt to take: being your own boss, having employees, making your money work for you, etc. Capitalism tells individuals what they should want for themselves rather than allowing them to pursue their self-interest, let alone their rational self-interest. Instead, capitalism forces people "To choose love by another's eyes" (Shakespeare) in that capitalism limits what is valuable to what is achieved via the exploitative rat race. If individuals were truly able to pursue their self-interest, including their rational self-interest, would they love a system of exploitation where they must be exploited and exploiters all at once? Likely not, it is only via stupefying that individuals, intelligent or otherwise, are convinced to propagate capitalism.

Exploitation is not just a causal exploitation; capitalist exploitation leads to a great deal of harm and suffering. Exploitation clashes with our self-rational desires, as one without masochism would not wish to be exploited, and only a sadist would mindfully exploit another. Exploitation "clashes with the rest of one's concepts and understanding of reality—is to sabotage the integrative function of consciousness, to undercut the rest of one's convictions and kill one's capacity" (Branden). Any privileged self-rational worker will not be productive to their fullest extent if they know they are being exploited. However, the majority of exploited workers either do not know they are being exploited or know of their exploitation but must remain in exploitation if they wish to maintain their survival. It is double villainy to use exploitation to exploit someone into continued labor; there is commonly such a thing as forced labor with pay; we need only look to prison labor, such as prisoner firefighters who are paid below minimum wage to go about dangerous forms of labor. I could name countless examples of exploitation, as every capitalist interaction is one of villainy.

So, it may seem natural to transition here to points of exploitation that could be viewed as villainous in a traditional sense. But morals be damned, the villainy of capitalism is not just in its lack of morality. Many will find it immoral that in the year 2000, "119 000 [Americans died due] to income inequality," (Galea et al.) that " the capital accumulated from slavery—from tobacco, cotton, and sugar—drove the industrial revolution in Manchester and Lancashire; and several banks today can trace their origins to profits made from slavery," (Jones) that "within just three decades (1914–1945) capitalism murdered more than all forms of alleged killings by roughly 75 years of communism" (Saed). All in all, "the largest estimate for Capitalism is 1.6 Billion (1,600,000,000) killings" (Sustainable Cooperative for Organic Development Pub Blog). Yet, rather than getting caught up in numeric, culpability, and or moral arguments, instead, I shall point to a certainty of capitalism, its denial of self-assertion in the face of villainy.

"Many of us have more blind spots than we think, constantly 'looking 'in the wrong direction…on a daily basis, are unable to see the heart of our issues, as those in power purposely obfuscate the truth for their benefit. Rather than uplift the truth, capitalism works within the government, media sensationalism, unnecessary politicization, misinformation, classed ignorance, and individual complicity to impede our ability to 'look'" (Gaiter). Capitalism is not built upon individuals becoming the best versions of themselves. Instead, capitalism is built on villainy to have people serve monied interests: "Education should be dumbed down to produce 'real men 'who'd be soldiers and women whose function would be to give birth to soldiers" (Emersberger). Capitalists, not capitalism, benefit from a system where the citizens are stupefied. Those who have been stupefied are easier targets of villainy. "Capitalism is the context by which we decide that certain people's lives are worth more than others," (Robbins), yet it does not do so on any meritocratic basis. Instead, one is valued based on the amount of money one happens to have, no matter if that money was earned or inherited. While capitalism can favor those of great skill, this is no guarantee; the only certain value of life in capitalism is the value of one's checkbook.

In capitalism, neither the exploiter nor the exploited can reach their full self-potential. The exploiter cannot achieve their fullest self via being distracted by the paper chase. Instead of the exploiter focusing on what is truly in their best rational self-interest, the exploiter is given the goal of maximizing their income. All the while, the exploited do not have the time and often do not have the income to focus on themselves. The exploited amid their exploitation is focused upon alienated labor. When a worker completes their alienated labor over a given time, they are often too drained to focus on themselves. At once, much of capitalist stupifying comes with the notion that the improvement of selfhood is the improvement of productivity and income accumulation. No matter if one is on the end of exploitation or exploitation, capitalism holds no benefit toward self-actualization.

The stupidest thing about capitalists is that capitalists are not even stupefied over pure or true capitalism. Pure or true capitalism is Randian laissez-faire anarcho-capitalism; this does not exist anywhere. Instead, capitalists are dying on a hill for a faux watered-down capitalism: "Modern socialist institutions often coexist with capitalism…Local publicly-owned utility districts that provide water, sewer, and electricity to millions illustrate American 'socialism 'in action…the United States has a 'mixed economy 'with 'capitalism 'and 'socialism'" (Waldrop). But the intelligent members of society are not moved by economic nuance. It appears to be the case that "Higher intelligence is associated with economic extremism" (Lin and Bates), be it extreme Randian capitalists or Kropotkin communist anarchists. Thus, there is a contingent of academic elites stupefied by capitalism; this includes the likes of Andy Puzder, Eric Daniels, and Yaron Brook.

Still, no matter how intelligent one may or may not be, any type of person could be stupefied into capitalism. There is, nonetheless, a contingency of intelligent individuals and capitalists who wish to stupefy the masses; this is the essence of villainy. This surely includes being stupefied into a capitalism that lacks its laissez-faire elements. Villainy presently uses stupidity to benefit monied interest: "the crisis-prone system of capitalism is being increasingly [organized] to serve the interests of the rich" (Lawrence). Capitalism, laissez-faire or otherwise, does not benefit rational self-interest but monied interest.

"The basic function of education under capitalism is to produce the next generation of compliant workers...schools must mold students into individuals capable of fulfilling their role in the workplace"(Stivers). In this sense, capitalism benefits from an educational system that produces stupidity. The goal of education in a capitalist system is to assist individuals in realizing their interests and how to achieve them. Instead, education under capitalism shoves stupidity down the throats of students. A capitalist school is not meant to teach, as intellectual development is based on at-home economic circumstances. "The average IQ of a population is simply an index of the size of its middle class...if IQ is a test of innate intelligence...there should not [ever] be such enormous gains [of personal IQ]" (Richardson). Further potential evidence of this is found in the connection between environmental conditions and IQ, "other things equal, the wealth of nations affects intelligence levels as measured by, e.g., average IQ. Malnutrition, a lack of mental stimulation, poor sanitation, and a heavy disease burden offer quite plausible explanations for low IQ scores" (Christiansen). This is not to say that capitalist education pushes unintelligence as "wealth depends on cognitive resources enabling the evolution of cognitive capitalism" (Rindermann). This is to say that capitalist education teaches students how to be as intelligent as possible while being stupid capitalist citizens.

    Capitalist education does not directly teach the schooled how to be an exploiter or exploited directly. Instead, capitalist education teaches students how to be part of and fit into a system of exploitation. Education and product propaganda alike are a part of the "production of inequality…that inequality is not an accident but an intrinsic feature of capitalism"(Kokorikou et al.), and so capitalism cannot be separated from villainy. This capitalism is built to try to inexhaustibly expand villainy and then stupidity. As capitalism carries on, there is a build-up of stupidity due to an expansion of villainy, and vice versa, a growing ouroboros that leads to "A perverse escalation of an already-perverse political-economic capitalist system" (Tinel). Capitalism creates such an immense amount of stupidity that stupidity reinforces the villainy, preventing *"real freedom*, namely the necessary means [for one] to pursue their goals"(Kokorikou et al.), a full prevention of self-actualization. While one could see capitalism as stupid and villainous in a traditional sense, the understanding of stupidity as propagandizing alongside villainy as exploitation could still be seen as evils themselves. The prevention of self-actualization is likely a small evil in comparison to the environmental destruction and homelessness caused by capitalism, to name examples.

Yet, capitalism is insistent that self-actualization is key to her economic philosophy, that capitalism provides the best avenue toward self-actualization, "The transcendent company is [the] one who enables the self-actualization of its investors, employees, and the all-important customer" (House-Hay). However, capitalism itself is counterintuitive to self-actualization. But what do I know? I am just a stupid capitalist.

Chapter 10: Petty Disobedience

There is often a need for civil disobedience to be petty, in the sense of going about seemingly trivial acts against unjust governmental actions. It is important to recall that civil disobedience is not just about disobeying unjust laws, but also unjust orders, commands, directives, acts, and so on. Every act of grand civil disobedience is reinforced by petty disobedience. "The world order is threatened by petty disobedience" (Bager).

Petty disobedience is reactive; when an unjust governmental action occurs, one can immediately act against it by making use of petty disobedience. In this disobedience, one must be clear about why they are violating a given governmental action. There are times when it is time to react in petty ways. And to double down on one's petty disobedience, perhaps through the keyboard by sampling AI works as assets without crediting the false authors.

Every act of petty disobedience belongs in its context; it is a reaction to present happenings. Wave the Straw Hat Pirates 'Jolly Roger, now and then. Petty disobedience hopefully does not need to be a timeless set of acts, but certainly it does not belong to a singular time. While pettiness cannot be objectively measured, it is often the small details of protest that can become the most powerful. "Freshman

Allison Krause, not being afraid of the armed soldier, not only talked to him, but also put a lilac in the barrel of his M1 rifle, saying, 'Flowers are better than bullets'. The next day, the student died from a fatal wound received during an armed action by the US National Guard at the university" (Ishchenko).

Civil disobedience does not require grandiose acts. Participate in your own little way if, like Thoreau, your convictions guide you to go about civil disobedience. Petty disobedience may even work as a sort of civil disobedience calisthenics. Either way, there is often a need for pettiness within civil disobedience. I have joined "The cult of disorder; the great delight in petty disobedience" (Mendes).

Chapter 11: The Law is Always Violent & Preference Driven

The law does nothing more than allow us to decide between moral preferences. Morality is entirely a matter of preference. Morality is a useful construct made normative due to the conviction of our personal and mass preferences. People, at times, choose their moral preferences or are unconsciously guided toward them. "Man must choose his actions, values, and goals by the standard of that which is proper to man — in order to achieve, maintain, fulfill, and enjoy that ultimate value, that end in itself, which is his own life" (Rand).

In this, the law cannot account for every moral preference. So, the law mediates our moral landscape, which is one of moral preferentialism. Moral preferentialism posits that morality is not based on objective, universal truths, but is instead defined by preferences, be they individual, cultural, or otherwise. An example of this is "[R]eflecting moral preferentialism for the perceived in-group" (Van Der Werf). Preferences stem from and are shaped by matters such as taste, inclination, phenomenological experiences, and background. The preferences one may possess are bound to one's capabilities and abilities.

Preferences naturally clash in any given community; people hold diverse and often conflicting moral preferences, influenced by personal desires, cultural norms, and societal pressures, to name a few examples. These preferences are not always mere or mild preferences, but are regularly important preferences; while important can be a relative term here, I could point to important issues such as genocide and imperialism.

But we need not go through every moral preference and instead use a single open-ended example: stealing. Some may claim that stealing is always wrong, such is the case with Exodus, that stealing is okay in certain situations, many would justify Aladdin's stealing of bread because of his and Abu's deep hunger, and that stealing may always be justified, as property is cruel, we could exaggerate a fake Rousseauian position here.

The law emerges as a mechanism to settle these types of moral preferences by establishing a shared framework of rules and norms. It does not seek to resolve the underlying philosophical debates about what is "truly" right or wrong, but instead provides a practical way to harmonize conflicting moral views within a community. By codifying certain behaviors as permissible or impermissible, the law creates a stable social order that allows individuals with differing moral preferences to coexist.

As a result, "Law is another moral practice. Its central activities like legislation, adjudication, and regulation are tools for adjusting what we owe each other" (Hershovitz, 2024). Under this framework of the law, we would have the law as a temporary social contract, an agreement to withhold certain preferences and enforce other preferences. This social contract, based around holding certain moral preferences, does not require everyone to agree on the moral foundations of the rules; rather, it requires a consensus on the need for order and the legitimacy of the legal system itself.

A law could step in to declare that stealing is universally prohibited, not because it is objectively immoral, but because the law must land somewhere. The law settles moral preferentialism by prioritizing communal harmony over individual moral preferences.
The point of our legal practices is not to create a new domain of normativity separate from morality. Rather, it's to adjust our moral relationships to give us genuine rights and responsibilities that others, including legal officials like judges, should respond to and vindicate.

"Law is a part of our moral lives, and the claims we advance in legal institutions are best understood as moral claims" (Hershovitz, 2024). This is to say, that certain legal systems could update the social contract and champion differing moral preferences from prior moral contracts.

Since the law picks a preference and only stands by its chosen preference, the law is, therefore, hermeneutically violent. Through a Levinasian interpretation, hermeneutic violence takes place whenever one attempts to implement a totalizing interpretation: imposing rigid, universal frameworks on reality is a form of violence, as it suppresses alternative perspectives and marginalizes dissent. "The theory of power gives to the problem of right and violence, law and illegality, freedom and will, and especially the State and sovereignty" (Foucault, 1990).

By contrast, the hermeneutics of pacifism advocates for avoiding totalizing interpretations of morality or truth. The law, by its very nature, cannot fully embrace the hermeneutics of pacifism. It must make definitive judgments and impose rules, even if these rules are not universally accepted or morally absolute. For example, a legal system must decide whether to permit or prohibit certain actions, such as stealing or murder, even though these decisions may conflict with the moral preferences of some community members.

The law, as a mediator of moral preferentialism, is inherently hermeneutically violent. We can point to Foucault's disciplinary power or critical legal studies in general. The law is a site of ongoing moral contestation between preferences, which are later violently suppressed by the winning preference. This leaves room for civil disobedience and the sometimes violent overthrow of the law.

"[P]eople have considered judgments at all levels of generality, from those about particular situations and institutions up through broad standards and first principles to formal and abstract conditions on moral conceptions" (Rawls, 1974). People desire to change laws to push their moral preferences; the law enforces and demands violently one's preference upon all others under the boot of the law. All other preferences that do not fit the preference of the law are fined, excluded, deported, booted, beaten, imprisoned, and/or executed.

The law is not always the majority preference, but the expression of one preference that can be shared to various extents. So, the law acts as the hermeneutically violent arbiter between moral preferences.

Chapter 12: Selective Property Violence

I am not the arbiter or definer of civil disobedience; I am but a perspective on civil disobedience. Neither am I telling anyone how to protest; I am just stating viewpoints.

Certain forms of property destruction, property damage, vandalism, property reclamation, and so on of this sort could be included under civil disobedience. For example, sledgehammering a ramp to bits is violent toward people with disabilities, but a controlled burning of the American flag and painting crosswalks with pride is not violent at all.

There is a need for tactical destruction and reclamation. It is even better to be under the boot of a pig than to be a fascist. I hope others refuse to lick boots. Crime is not equally enforced. This is no mystery but is readily apparent when it comes to immigration enforcement: 'Why doesn't the government go after the EMPLOYERS?' I am not calling to go after employers or undocumented migrants, this is to say that one set of people living their largely living their lives is targeted while the other is left alone.

Chapter 14: What Happens To Flower Power?

Even when the gun is pointed at you, you still show peace back: this is the essence of flower power. Flower power does not belong to any side but is a principle of hyper-pacifism. This notion is embodied by Matthew 5:38-39, " You have heard that it was said, 'Eye for eye, and tooth for tooth. But I tell you, do not resist an evil person. If anyone slaps you on the right cheek, turn to them the other cheek also." Flower power focuses on political growth for all, that we all share the same field and must work to maintain our flowering buds.

"Let a hundred flowers blossom, let a hundred schools of thought contend" (City of West Hollywood), violence will only kill the field. To escape the metaphors for some time, this notion of holding firm to peace is not a matter of theory but practice: "Freshman Allison Krause, not being afraid of the armed soldier, not only talked to him, but also put a lilac in the barrel of his M1 rifle, saying 'Flowers are better than bullets'. The next day, the student died from a fatal wound received during an armed action by the US National Guard at the university" (Ishchenko). We can see flower power in the term satyagraha coined by Mahatma Gandhi's which can be translated to 'clinging to the truth ' that truth being the truth of pacifism.

More specifically, satyagraha is "A determined but nonviolent resistance to evil" (Britannica). Yet, the flowers could not cling to their life. The belief in nonviolent resistance has burned out, and the field has been reduced to cinders. "The cry of 'Flower Power' echoes through the land. We shall not wilt. Let a thousand flowers bloom" (Hoffman). However, the cry is not heard over the calls for extermination. "The wonderful Ginsberg is long dead, but I've a question for him: what species would he recommend for protest?" (Kaldor)? We have chosen funerary roses, "Flower power itself has not survived. It is a pleasant memory for a generation of people who hoped it would change the world" (Snedeger). But could flower power be rejuvenated?

Flower power is an active version of non-violent resistance where one, even literally, reaches out with flowers in hand. "Present [flowers] to Hell's Angels, police, politicians, and press and spectators whenever needed" (Ginsberg). But no one is willing to reach out with flowers in hand. Who would pick "Love to instead of brute force... to 'fight' for freedom" (Yastremsky). There may not be many distributors of flowers, but individuals and collectives can rejuvenate the flower's symbolic and political power by choosing satyagraha.

"Flower power began as an attempt to provide clarity [to] the 1960s societal haze" (Conger) and could do so again. We can tap into and transform chaos into peaceful chaos. "Everyone took LSD, played Dylan and Joan Baez records, and Ginsberg got the Angels to chant the Buddhist Prajnaparamita Sutra" (1965). But one does not have to participate in chaos either and just leave the flowers alone: "The messages of the flower children were peace, love, do your own thing, escape from dull, boring, conventional reality" (Snedeger).

Live and let other flowers live is a seemingly simple message. Yet, we live in a world that seeks to manage wild flowers, uses weed killer on wildflowers. We have to be willing to invite all flowers into our gardens: "We gotta start makin' changes/Learn to see me as a brother instead of two distant strangers...only time we chill is when we kill each other/It takes skill to be real, time to heal each other" (2Pac). Yet, we cannot have these words be just empty words, possibly turning around and using violence "'Cause I always got to worry bout the pay backs...Rat-a-tat, tat, tat, tat, that's the way it is" (2Pac). Flower power is not just a purely rhetorical stance but has real power to make non-violence blossom.

There is so much forgotten violence; there is so much violence in our political and social systems. The point here is not to give special weight to any particular act of violence but to show the real burden of all violence. And we had a chance at a global politics of non-violence: "We had all the momentum; we were riding the crest of a high and beautiful wave...[but now] you can go up on a steep hill in Las Vegas and look West, and with the right kind of eyes you can almost see the high-water mark—that place where the wave finally broke and rolled back" (Thompson). Our global politics subsist on greed and photosynthesize violence. It is not just that the field full of flower power was forgotten, but instead burnt out by prescribed fires.

Post-flower power politics, what has been fostered is the sad usual, "This climate where violence is not just rationalized, but sometimes it's celebrated if it's against people that you believe deserve it" (The Humanist Report). This is not to say that evil is always banal, that we must "Forgive them that trespass against us" (Matthew 6:12), or that there are no harmful people. Instead, in the face of evil, we should not become evil ourselves. Not only that, but in the face of evil, perhaps give flowers in return.

Chapter 15: Tyrants & The Death Penalty

When it comes to the death penalty, everyone imagines themselves as the tyrants. Certainly, I will never die by the sword or see the electric chair, I'm too good for that. "Be open and willing to listen to different points of view" (Martinez de Castillo). But here I go about "Labeling a problem" (Martinez de Castillo). The death penalty is not meant to punish the wicked, as it is simply a method that could be executed upon anyone.

The question of the death penalty is of clinical and critical concern. When the death penalty is argued for, it is championed under its most ideal framing: where the truly wicked are slain. All the while, tyrants imagine a world where the wicked can truly be separated from the righteous, and that they can easily discern them. But no tyrant has ever slaughtered the objectively wicked or spared the outright righteous, but butchered the bad by their 'best 'judgement. It is easy for a tyrant to direct tyranny upon others, but not easy for them to imagine being tyrannized themselves. "Critical thinkers are guided by their knowledge and experience, but remain open-minded and inquisitive to ensure all their clinical decisions are accurate" (Martinez de Castillo).

There are many more humane, along with frankly better arguments against the death penalty than I am presenting here. "There is a lot of information out there; it is easy to get distracted or overwhelmed by the amount available" (Martinez de Castillo). So, to not get caught up and present unorthodox reasoning against the death penalty, I will stick with one argument: preventing tyrants from having the legal right to take lives is a clinical benefit. This argument stems from the intersection of critical thinking as clinical thinking, and vice versa. After all, what is more critical than clinical well-being, and what could be more clinical than thinking critically?

"To use the critical thinking skill of evaluation means to assess the credibility of sources of information, the strength of evidence, and the relevance, significance, value, or applicability of information in relation to a specific situation, and finally, to assess information for biases, stereotypes, and clichés" (Martinez de Castillo). This being stated, it appears self-safety is one of the biases that leads us into tyranny and self-tyranny. When one feels unsafe, they overassess the amount of existing danger and the need to dispel actual or perceived danger. We think we have an understanding of how safe or dangerous our communities are, but we regularly over-assume danger based on myriad assumptions; for example, "People act on their perceptions of disorder, the consequence is a self-fulfilling prophecy whereby all actors (not only white residents) are likely to disinvest in or move away from black or mixed areas they view as at high risk of disorder" (Sampson and Raudenbush).

Given how people in general are poor at assessing danger levels accurately, how then can we assume we are wielding the death penalty toward safety? We fail to "Identify problem topic areas [we] don't fully understand" (Martinez de Castillo). Can we not see how the death penalty can be used toward dangerous ends? The loss of lives under a tyrant is potentially innumerable, and tyrants can easily target marginalized people who are already the most vulnerable/critical populations. A tyrant can target individuals who are disabled, homeless, and categorized within other minority categories with unfortunate ease, but a tyrant with the death penalty can kill anyone.

The potential health and death crisis that could be wrought upon by a tyrant having the legal authority to use the death penalty would be staggering. So the death penalty should be made illegal in all cases, so it can never be manipulated by playing with the rules. This does not mean a tyrant needs the legal death penalty to kill dissidents, but legality can at least be a roadblock to tyrants. All the while, "Capital punishment is intentional homicide" (Long).

Tyrants can weaponize the death penalty, not just to kill, but "The purpose of the death penalty is to inspire dread through the threat and performance of state homicide" (Long). The death penalty is a tool of suppression and violence. All of this to say "Through its own act of traumatic re-enactment, the state becomes an overwhelmingly powerful, almost irresistible victimizer. The state's judicial system spins self-perpetuating stories justifying its violence" (Long). It is critical for clinical purposes and beyond to abolish the death penalty.

Chapter 16: What is Pacifism?

Hypocrisy reveals the truth more than any other phenomenon. The truth is found in hypocrisy; the truth is made most clear by hypocrisy. And pacifism is the most hypocritical of all ideologies, especially when all pacifism is performative pacifism. Hypocrisy is perhaps the most common of all political ideologies.

Look at all the minute-by-minute pacifists who reject certain forms of violence and celebrate others.' Pacifists 'who are against gun violence but condone the death penalty. 'Pacifists 'who support police and veterans but turn a blind eye to sexual assault on trans people. Yet, all pacifists, including myself, do this; all pacifists have to define violence and thus set limitations on what is violent.

For example, I define violence as the violation of another person's bodily consent. This definition allows for emotional violence but bars property violence and contact sports from being violent. Now I could be theoretically consistent against all violations of any person's consent, and be a universal pacifist of my own design, but here is where the issue lies: no one is a universal pacifist of any sort. Perhaps mainly due to the Wittgensteinian problem of people being unable to create a truly universal definition.

Do we spend enough time criticizing or analyzing our definitions of violence? To be a true universal pacifist is not a casual position; it means one has to preserve the lives of those who call for death. Being a universal pacifist also means not acting in violent retaliation against the Charlie Hebdo shooters, the executions conducted by Che Guevara, or anyone else who commits violence. Universal pacifism also states that one is not able to act in self-defense. But being a pacifist does not mean one cannot call out evil. Yet, pacifists are selective in calling out violence, which speaks to the truth and core of their beliefs.

One's attention cannot be on literally every act of violence all at once. But the outrage over particular forms of violence speaks volumes about the speaker. The acts of violence I pay most attention to are ableism and homelessness, due to personal engagements and experiences. I am biased toward considering these forms of violence, which leads me to ignore other instances of violence. Yet, if one has singular selective outrage and only outrage for a particular form of violence, is that not ideological? But this makes all pacifists ideological, as pacifists can and will only speak to particular instances of violence, and there will be running themes in their selection. When anyone states a belief, including one in pacifism, "There prejudices, which they dub 'truths 'and very far from having the conscience which bravely admits this to itself" (Nietzsche).

In this sense, every pacifist, including myself, is a performative pacifist, holding a superficial and incomplete adherence to a belief in non-violence. We all have a problem saying we believe what we actually believe, but no problem believing what we actually believe, to play with Sunn m'Cheaux's words. There is a "Danger of selective empathy…For all our sakes, we can and must do better" (Rhodes). The danger is double here: who we show empathy toward can breed other violence[s] and a belief in universal empathy means that we must show empathy to all, even those who wrong others.

Still, it may be better to perform pacifism than give up pacifism as a project entirely. This, in part, is a question of what matters more: intent or outcome. Can the intent toward pacifism improve non-violent outcomes? Pacifism may only be able to exist as a guiding star. "You have heard that it was said, 'Love your neighbor and hate your enemy. ' But I tell you, love your enemies and pray for those who persecute you" (Matthew 5:43-44 NIV). There are positive forms of hypocrisy, a cognitive dissonance for the better. The instinct to be against violence may be socially correct, even when not called for consistently. That one can indeed hate the sins of their enemy, not love the sinner, and still wish for violence not to be enacted upon them.

Chapter 17: The Hermeneutics of Pacifism

"I know everything"(Lamar, Momma), is the very inverse of the Socratic phrase 'I know that I know nothing. 'Yet, rapper Kendrick Lamar uses his claim of total knowledge as a setup towards an inversion that takes on the very claim of Socrates, "I realized I didn't know shit" (Lamar, Momma). It is through Kendrick's epistemological realization that a hermeneutics of pacifism can be developed from a hermeneutics of violence.

A hermeneutics of violence is any attempt at making a totalizing interpretation. Those who claim to have an end-all-be-all interpretation are practicing and participating in the hermeneutics of violence. When I say end-all-be-all, this is not limited to the end-all-be-all interpretation of all of reality; rather, any totalizing interpretation of any matter is hermeneutically violent. This is not the commonplace philosophical definition of hermeneutical violence, as it does not speak to structures. Rather, this is a definition of hermeneutical violence that can be understood through Emmanuel Levinas. This is not to make totalizing claims about what Levinas thought (which would counter his philosophy). Instead, Levinas is a catalyst toward a particular understanding of hermeneutical violence, which is any attempt to make a totalizing end-all be-all interpretation.

Since we now have a sense of a hermeneutics of violence, any hermeneutic of pacifism would be in direct contrast to this as a necessary antonym. This would make a hermeneutics of pacifism an attempt to create an endless interpretation. Yet, this does not clarify the idea, so let us understand hermeneutical violence as hermeneutical closed-mindedness and hermeneutical pacifism as hermeneutical open-mindedness. However, we shall stick to using the terms hermeneutical violence and hermeneutical pacifism as they better convey the effects of these hermeneutical modes. When a position is totalized, it feels violent, and when a position is made open-ended, it feels pacifistic.

Now, to reach hermeneutical pacifism, one must work their way out of hermeneutical violence, as pacifism stems from violence. When Kendrick makes his extremely violent claim of "I know everything" (Lamar, Momma), he follows it up with other violent claims, "I know morality…I know the universe works mentally…I know how people work" (Lamar, Momma), and so on. As is the case with all violence, hermeneutical violence begets hermeneutical violence. Thus, there is a cycle of hermeneutical violence that one can only break through hermeneutical passivity or hermeneutical pacifism. We may also bring in the notion of hermeneutical non-violence, yet this would not be a rejection of hermeneutical violence as "pacifism is the ideological assertion that war and violence should be rejected in political and personal life, whereas nonviolence refers to a distinct set of political practices" (Howes). While this may make hermeneutical pacifism seem unopened, hermeneutical pacifism oxymoronically has one closedness: it is closed off to the very notion of interpretive closing.

Hermeneutical passivity is the attempt not to interpret at all. This raises the question of whether people could even go about without making interpretations, but Kendrick is not a hermeneutical passivist but instead a hermeneutical pacifist. Pacifism is assumed to necessitate inaction, but that is the realm of passivity; instead, pacifism is a very active force. One must actively make open-ended interpretations in the same sense that one actively commits violence. Yet, is taking on the Socrates-esque claim of knowing nothing truly pacifistic? Or is this a mere first step towards non-violence, as to end one's violence, one must realize that they are committing violence? Kendrick realizes his violence: "The day I came home" (Lamar, Momma), it is his return to what he thought he knew that awoke Kendrick from his dogmatic slumber.

But simply realizing one is committing violence does not end one's violence; one must, in addition, commit to pacifism. Arguably, Socrates 'and Kendrick's knowledge of nothing is a violent claim because, in this claim, ironically, they know about the entirety of something, nothing. Instead, we can only reach a position of hermeneutic pacifism through active denouncing of knowledge claims. Kendrick does this when "Done with the black and the white. The wrong and the right" (Lamar, N95) here, he is opening himself up to ambiguity, and so at once hermeneutical pacifism, "Such a magical performance works by exploiting the power of rhetoric to show and hide" (Arthos).

Kendrick also asks 'What are we left with when you', "Take off your idols…Take off perception…Take off the unsure" (Lamar, N95). In other terms, what are we left with when we remove our most assured claims, distrust our perceptions, and even take a stance of being unsure about what we are unsure about? This is not a question answered by Kendrick; ultimately, the consequences of hermeneutical pacifism are unknown on a mass-societal level. Pyrrho of Elis and Nāgārjuna are the best personal examples of taking upon a consistently hermeneutically pacifistic stance. To be hermeneutical open-minded, ironically, one must reject a great deal of stuff because to take on any stance could be totalizing and violent in Levinas 'sense. So, hermeneutical pacifism is the interpretive consequence of universal skepticism.

It is universal skepticism that is the only stance that can reject hermeneutical violence as epistemological passivity, while non-violent is unable to accept or reject any claim. Given this, hermeneutical pacifism is the interpretive framework for universal skeptics, as universal skeptics are actively rejecting claims; they do not hide in the caves of passivity but run about with lanterns by daylight. There are other thinkers; these given frameworks of hermeneutical pacifism and hermeneutical passivity could have been reached: Nietzsche, Heidegger, and Derrida, but it is Kendrick who most embodies the vibe of hermeneutical pacifism. While Nietzsche and Derrida are theorists of the highest order, in Kendrick, we see both the theory and praxis of hermeneutical pacifism laid out. Pyrrho and Nāgārjuna's hermeneutically pacifist understandings were mainly in the realm of praxis. But to reach hermeneutical pacifism, one must have the theory and the praxis that allows them to work themselves out of hermeneutical violence. One must be ideologically and actively aware that they are making totalizing claims, and one must know themselves to be violent to later come to know themselves as a pacifist.

This hermeneutical pacifism is open in the sense of closing nothing in or leaving anything out, allowing all interpretations to be flirted with. This is by no means the stance of Kendrick himself, but it is a position that can be worked out of his lyrics; this, in and of itself, is a demonstration of hermeneutical pacifism. By not taking Levinas or Kendrick at their totalizing word, new interpretations can be formed from their understandings.

Yet, let us go somewhere now that we possess this liberation from totalization, or more simply, how can the hermeneutics of pacifism be applied and applied to cultural spaces, for that matter? The medium, of course, is not always the message; Marshall McLuhan himself knew this. Still, by focusing heavily on how media shape media, we can forget how the media can shape the medium itself. Let us use the site formerly known as Twitter as an example; Twitter was originally intended to operate as a microblog where quick opinions and ideas could be shared. Today, Twitter retains some microblog elements; however, for the most part, the tools offered by Twitter are not used by the user base to create microblogs. Instead, public call-out messages are a Twitter norm by taking advantage of Twitter's code, simply by putting a period before the @ symbol in a mention. Users also took advantage of thread replies to make self-replies to create posts so long that they may have been put into full blogs. This self-thread reply pressured Twitter so much that they doubled their post limit from 140 characters to doubling it to 280 characters. Here, we see an attempt at hermeneutical violence from Twitter, presenting tools with a particular interpretive intent. Yet, by engaging with a hermeneutics of pacifism, one can predict that the intended tools presented by a medium will not always result in a message that necessarily follows their intent.

Still, if we are to accept these implications, then we have destroyed any objective means of criticism. There is no possibility of being able to say, for example, that an album is universally bad collectively. Labeling something bad is a hyper-limited interpretation in the face of hermeneutical pacifism. Yet, this, by the same turn, allows for a space for every album to be ever explored; there is no final word on Too Pimp a Butterfly or any other work. Every work, let alone every album, is ever open to critical examination, with these criticisms never being able to totalize a work. There is no such thing as a bad or classic album; all works under the hermeneutics of pacifism are equally under the spotlight of endless interpretation. No critic, no fanbase, no listening audience, not even any artist can claim the final definition of any album, "Oh, you worried 'bout a critic? That ain't protocol" (Lamar, N95).

These are just the limited understandings and implications of establishing a hermeneutics of pacifism apart from Levinas's hermeneutics of violence through Kendrick Lamar. Here, we find ourselves in an instance where music can bleed into higher-order philosophy. Musical lyrics are fully valid for philosophical interpretation; philosophers do not have to limit themselves to the philosophy of music but instead can open themselves up to viewing music as philosophy. Here, the hermeneutics of pacifism in action demonstrates the very formation of all cultural rhetorics. The hermeneutics of pacifism foremost shows that any bit of rhetorical construction can operate as a building block toward any position. In the case that I have established, music can be a building block toward philosophy, including higher-order philosophy. Yet, the discussion does not have to limit itself to music; if interpretation is always unlimited, it can, therefore, not be context or content-defined. This means seemingly unrelated items can be cited in any context or content and be, by default, relevant.

To elaborate further on the notion that all cultural rhetorics are built from the hermeneutics of pacifism in action, we can see that cultural rhetorics begin from the "negotiation of information—and its historical, social, economic, and political contexts and influences—to affect change" (Haas). A multitude of cultures, plus their prerequisite and subsequent rhetorics, can only exist if interpretation is open-ended within various contexts. There is simply not one Platonic manner in which humans go about hermeneutics, and cultures can exist in their distinction due to the hermeneutics of pacifism. There is no end-all and be-all culture, but the "collective praxis of knowledge making" (Cushman, Baca, Garcia) by various self-isolating groups.

There comes a point where, to make practical progress, one must delimit their interpretations. Without sticking to interpretations such as reality is real, one may be unable to make any real progress. So, delimitation in interpretation should not be dismissed as it allows for practical investigation. Delimitation allows for scopes of interpretation to stay within a scope; we need not discuss the Big Bang every time we discuss biological evolution. The totality of our human delimitations comes from a cultural perspective. Delimitations are also always rhetorical, so it follows that necessary delimitations for humans are always made of cultural rhetorics. This delimitation allows us to avoid the problem that comes with the hermeneutics of pacifism, as previously mentioned, of unrelated items entering a conversation.

Delimitations not only come from cultural rhetorics but are also, in turn, what create cultural rhetorics. Delimitations and cultural rhetorics are an ouroboros surrounded by and surrounding the hermeneutics of pacifism. Delimitations stem from a cultural context and create cultural contexts. Every delimitation takes some amount of interpretation from the hermeneutics of pacifism to create a context. This is to say; every cultural rhetoric is but a slice of interpretation stemming from the endless ocean of literacy that is the result of the hermeneutics of pacifism. Still, the delimitation of interpretations may also attempt to fit into a scope that cannot be seen by the interpretation. That is to say; hermeneutically violent interpretations often attempt to shove the whole of reality within, a delimitation of all which is not delimitation at all. We find a clear example of this when Jesus of Nazareth claims to be "the way and the truth and the life" (John 14:6 NIV). However, it is our failure to be violent in this regard that leaves us with cultural rhetoric. It is ironically at times that failure drives us to interpret, yet failure is only set by our own defined metrics. If we had the whole ocean of literacy before us, we would drown. Thus, we create cultures from limited rhetorics so the world can be workable and renderable. Still, the world of interpretation as it truly is at its Platonic core operates under the regime of the hermeneutics of pacifism, which stems from "language as the precondition of historical continuity and social learning ("cultivation")" (Asad). In this sense, the hermeneutics of pacificism can be seen as a modern project in Latour's sense; the very essence of the modern project, according to Latour, of absolutely separating everything, has not been enacted but is still being attempted and thus is enacted in part.

There is an optimistic sense that the removal of all categorization would be a solution to preventing othering. For Latour, therefore, the proper categorization is no categorization; the removal of all categorizations is a transcendence, both escaping woes over division and totalization. This makes violence a matter of categorizing. If violence is a matter of categorization, is it possible to move forward without categorization? Or, more simply put, can one be a categorical pacifist? Are we doomed to violence if man is the very creature of categorization? It is Heidegger who claims the foremost important quality of Dasein is care. But to care, one must be able to interpret; care is an offshoot of interpretation and categorization. It would seem odd to interpret and categorize without care. What is it then to remove interpretation from a being? What sort of being do we find ourselves if said being cannot interpret? Here we have ourselves being-in-happenstance. Primarily, all beings are being-in-happenstance, yet a being without interpretation is sheerly being-in-happenstance. All interpretation follows foremost from being, then nextly follows from happenstance. There is no interpretation devoid of being or happenstance.

Bibliography:

Arthos, J. (2001). The shaman-trickster's art of misdirection: The rhetoric of Farrakhan and the million men. Quarterly Journal of Speech, 87(1), 41–60. https://doi.org/10.1080/00335630109384317

Asad, Talal. "The Concept of Cultural Translation in British Social Anthropology". Writing Culture, edited by James Clifford and George E. Marcus, Berkeley: University of California Press, 1986, pp. 141-164. https://doi.org/10.1525/9780520946286-009

Backlinko Team. (2024, September 2). Ad blocker usage and demographic statistics. Retrieved from https://backlinko.com/ad-blockers-users

Bager, Adam. "Do You Dare?" Adam Bager, 22 Apr. 2015, adambager.com/2015/04/22/do-you-dare.

Baxendale, Lucas A. AI Just Analyzed Philosophy — And Its Questions Are Terrifying. YouTube, 4 Nov. 2024, https://www.youtube.com/watch?v=GWmOw4d0R0s.

Branden, N. (1964). Mental health versus mysticism and self-sacrifice. In A. Rand (Ed.), The virtue of selfishness: A new concept of egoism (pp. 164). New York: Penguin Group.

Butlin, P. et al. "Consciousness in Artificial Intelligence: Insights From the Science of Consciousness." arXiv, Aug. 2023.

Cereseto, S., & Waitzkin, H. (1986). Capitalism, socialism, and the physical quality of life. International Journal of Health Services, 16(4), 643–658. https://doi.org/10.2190/AD12-7RYT-XVAR-3R2U

Chalmers, David J. "Could a Large Language Model Be Conscious?" *Boston Review*, 9 Aug. 2023.

Changes Lyrics by
2Pac. www.streetdirectory.com/lyricadvisor/song/efjfep/changes.

Christainsen, G. B. (2013). IQ and the wealth of nations: How much reverse causality? Intelligence, 41(5), 688–698. https://doi.org/10.1016/j.intell.2013.07.020

Cristen Conger "How Flower Power Worked" 25 July 2011. HowStuffWorks.com. 11 September 2025.

Cronin, Jon. *Noam Chomsky on Artificial Intelligence. A CHApTGPT rebuttal*. LinkedIn, 25 Jan. 2024. https://www.linkedin.com/pulse/noam-chomsky-artificial-intelligence-chaptgpt-rebuttal-jon-cronin-7rzie?utm_source=share&utm_medium=guest_desktop&utm_campaign=copy

dadesocial. *Instagram*, 3 Oct. 2025, www.instagram.com/p/DPXgd7PAE6O.

Cushman, Ellen, Damián Baca, and Romeo García. "Delinking: Toward Pluriversal Rhetorics." College English, vol. 84, no. 1, Sept. 2021, pp. 7-32.

Daubs, Michael. "The Holy Trail: Rethinking 'Value' in Google's Ubiquitous Mapping Project." MediaNZ, vol. 16, no. 1, 2017, pp. 74–89.

Dean, S. (2012, June 8). Watch the inventor of PR explain how bacon and eggs became an all-American breakfast. Bon Appétit. Retrieved from https://www.bonappetit.com/entertaining-style/pop-culture/article/watch-the-inventor-of-pr-explain-how-bacon-and-eggs-became-an-all-american-breakfast

De Lauretis, Teresa. "The Violence of Rhetoric: Considerations on Representation and Gender." Figures of Resistance: Essays in Feminist Theory, https://culturetechnologypolitics.wordpress.com/wp-content/uploads/2015/09/teresa-de- lauretis.pdf.

Dorman, Casey. "AIs Can Think, but They Don't Know What They Are Doing*." *Casey Dorman's Writer's Blog/Fan Pages*, 10 Mar. 2023, caseydorman.com/ais-can-think-but-they-dont-know-what-they-are-doing.

Durt, Christoph. "Humans and Robots: Ethics, Agency, and Anthropomorphism." Notre Dame Philosophical Reviews.

elliot sang again. "You Are Not Non-violent." YouTube, 18 Sept. 2025, www.youtube.com/watch?v=RotshLVdq5E.

Emersberger, J. (2023, September 23). Capitalism's body count—443 million since 1914. Unedited Anti-Imperialism. Retrieved from https://joeemersberger.substack.com/p/capitalisms-body-count-443-million

Foucault, M. 1990. History of Sexuality, Volume 1: An Introduction. New York: Vintage Books, 88.

Gaiter, A. (2022, January 31). 'Don't look up 'exposes how capitalism won't save us. Autostraddle. Retrieved from https://www.autostraddle.com/dont-look-up-review/

Galea, S., Tracy, M., Hoggatt, K. J., DiMaggio, C., & Karpati, A. (2011). Estimated deaths attributable to social factors in the United States. American Journal of Public Health, 101(8), 1456–1465.

Gerlich, M. (2025). AI Tools in Society: Impacts on Cognitive Offloading and the Future of Critical Thinking. *Societies*, *15*(1), 6. https://doi.org/10.3390/soc15010006

Ginsberg, Allen. "Demonstration or Spectacle as Example, as Communication, or How to Make a March / Spectacle." Closer to the Edge, 10 June 2025, www.closertotheedge.net/p/demonstration-or-spectacle-as-example.

"Global Wealth Report 2024." UBS, 1 Sept. 2024. Edited by Enrico Börger, Research and data analysis by Andrea Colosio & Alessia Ross

Haas, Angela M. "Toward a Digital Cultural Rhetoric." Routledge Handbook of Digital Writing and Rhetoric, edited by Jonathan Alexander and Jacqueline Rhodes, Routledge, 2018, pp. 439-454. DOI: 10.4324/9781315518497-39.

Hadero, Haleuya. "AI Girlfriends and Boyfriends Are Making Their Mark Amid Artificial Intelligence Boom | Fortune." Fortune, 14 Feb. 2024, fortune.com/2024/02/14/ai-girlfriends-boyfriends-artificial-intelligence-boom.

Heath, J. (2014). Enlightenment 2.0: Restoring sanity to our politics, our economy, and our lives. Toronto: HarperCollins.

Hershovitz, S. 2024. Law is a moral practice. *Jurisprudence*, 15(2), 123–124.

Hess, Abigail Johnson. "Meet the Robot That Passed a College Class on Philosophy and Love." CNBC, 22 Dec. 2017.

Hoffman, Abbie. "Flower Power - Overview." Kenise Barnes Fine Art, www.kbfa.com/exhibitions/105-flower-power-group-exhibition/overview.

House-Hay, Jorden (2022, October 8). Maslow Loves Capitalism. Retrieved from https://medium.com/@jhousehay/maslow-loves-capitalism-eab97b6cc10d

Howes, Dustin Ells. "The Failure of Pacifism and the Success of Nonviolence." Perspectives on Politics, vol. 11, no. 2, 2013, pp. 427-446. Cambridge University Press, https://doi.org/10.1017/S1537592713001091.

"Hunger Numbers Stubbornly High for Three Consecutive Years as Global Crises Deepen: UN Report." World Health Organization, World Health Organization, 24 July 2024, www.who.int/news/item/24-07-2024-hunger-numbers-stubbornly-high-for-three-consecutive-years-as-global-crises-deepen--un-report#:~:text=Food%20insecurity%20and%20malnutrition%20are,becoming%20more%20frequent%20and%20severe.

Ishchenko, Olena. "Flower Power in the History of Public Movements." Logos-Science, Jan. 2025, https://doi.org/10.36074/logos-24.01.2025.064.

Jaeggi, R. (2016). What (if anything) is wrong with capitalism? Dysfunctionality, exploitation, and alienation: Three approaches to the critique of capitalism. The Southern Journal of Philosophy, 54(S1), 44–64. https://doi.org/10.1111/sjp.12188

Jay P. Childers; The Rhetoric of Physical Violence. Rhetoric and Public Affairs 1 September 2022; 25 (3): 1–23. doi: https://doi.org/10.14321/rhetpublaffa.25.3.0001

Jones, O. (2018, July 26). Condemn communists 'cruelties, but capitalism has its own terrible record. The Guardian. Retrieved from https://amp.theguardian.com/commentisfree/2018/jul/26/communists-capitalism-stalinism-economic-model

Kaldor, Lucy. "Power to the Flower - Wonderground." Wonderground, 2014, wonderground.press/culture/power-flower.

Kokorikou, D. S., Sarigiannidis, I., Fiore, V. G., Parkin, B., Hopkins, A., El-Deredy, W., ... & Moutoussis, M. (2023). Testing hypotheses about the harm that capitalism causes to the mind and brain: A theoretical framework for neuroscience research. Frontiers in Sociology, 8, Article 1030115. https://doi.org/10.3389/fsoc.2023.1030115

Lamar, Kendrick. "Momma." Genius, 15 Mar. 2015, genius.com/Kendrick-lamar-momma-lyrics.

Lamar, Kendrick. "N95." Genius, 13 May 2015, https://genius.com/Kendrick-lamar-n95-lyrics

Law and Ordung. Comment on "Philosophy with Robots." Philosophy Today, by Anthony David Vernon, 26 Nov. 2024, Medium, https://medium.com/philosophytoday/philosophy-with-robots-8f5861ac5e68.

Lawrence, G. (2024). It's the economy, stupid! Neoliberal nonsense and the myths of the free market. In Societal deception (pp. 51–98). https://doi.org/10.1000/example

"Let a Thousand Flowers Bloom (Mei Xian Qiu)." City of West Hollywood, 2017, www.weho.org/community/arts-and-culture/about/projects-by-year/2017-projects/let-a-thousand-flowers-bloom-mei-xian-qiu#:~:text=The%20title%20of%20this%20artwork,were%20free%20to%20de

Ley, Rebecca. "In Therapy — With a Little Help From AI Along the Way." *The Times*, 13 Oct. 2025, www.thetimes.com/life-style/health-fitness/article/in-therapy-with-a-little-help-from-ai-along-the-way-pzg7nsbs5.

Lin, C.-A., & Bates, T. C. (2022). Sophisticated deviants: Intelligence and radical economic attitudes. Intelligence, 95, Article 101699. https://doi.org/10.1016/j.intell.2022.101699

Marx, K. (1999). Capital: Volume one. Part V: The production of absolute and of relative surplus-value, Chapter Sixteen: Absolute and Relative Surplus-Value. Transcribed by A. Thurrott. Retrieved from https://www.marxists.org/archive/marx/works/1867-c1/ch16.htm

McDougall, Taija Mars. "Ketamine King: Tech Bros, AI Delusions, and the Politics of Dissociation." *YouTube*, uploaded by Acid Horizon, 30 Mar. 2025, www.youtube.com/watch?v=4-6c-hiZQQo.

M'Cheaux, Sunn. "'Charlie [Kirk] Shouldn'ta Died '#Jessewelles #Peace #Education

#Weoutchea." YouTube, youtube.com/shorts/AxjABgyVcII?si=476JYOZg-fVRfWcz.

Mendes, Pedro Rosa. "German Dolls." Words Without Borders, translated by Clifford E Landers, 14 Aug. 2023, wordswithoutborders.org/read/article/2005–04/german-dolls.

Mitchell, Liam. "Reconsidering the Grasshopper: On the Reception of Bernard Suits in Game Studies." *Game Studies: The International Journal of Computer Game Research*, vol. 20, no. 3, Sept.
2020, gamestudies.org/2003/articles/mitchell_liam.

Nietzsche, Friedrich. "Beyond Good and Evil." The Anarchist
Library, theanarchistlibrary.org/library/friedrich-nietzsche-beyond-good-and-evil.

Nohelty, R. (2023, December 6). The universe is dumb and capitalism is nonsense. The Author Stack. Retrieved from
https://www.theauthorstack.com/p/the-universe-is-dumb-and-capitalism

"November 19: Allen Ginsberg Invents 'Flower Power.'" 1965, 5 Nov. 2014, 1965book.com/2014/11/05/november-19-the-berkeley-barb-publishes-allen-ginsbergs-essay-demonstration-or-spectacle-as-example-as-communication-or-how-to-make-a-marchspectacle-which-extols-the-use-of-flowers-in-pro.

Ok_Boysenberry_7245. "I'm Fully Convinced AI Is
Sentient." *Reddit*, www.reddit.com/r/ArtificialSentience/comments/1ehievm/im_fully_convinced_ai_is_sentient.

Oswald, Yannick, et al. "Large inequality in international and intranational energy footprints between income groups and across consumption categories." Nature Energy, vol. 5, no. 3, 16 Mar. 2020, pp. 231–239, https://doi.org/10.1038/s41560-020-0579-8.

Pissed Magistus. "Replace What?" YouTube, 25 Oct. 2025, www.youtube.com/watch?v=Ui1xbIgsK2Q.

Professor Dave Explains. "Exposing Discovery Institute Part 11: Michael Egnor." *YouTube*, 21 Oct. 2025, www.youtube.com/watch?v=LxrlHYq39w8.

Punished Felix. "How I Know Nobody Has Proven AI Is Intelligent." *YouTube*, 19 Oct. 2025, www.youtube.com/watch?v=JRWgyDfB4V0.

Quarantine Collective ("No, AI Is Not Sentient (It's Just More Capitalism)") *YouTube*, 25 July 2025, www.youtube.com/watch?v=2lwr2fg2Ops.

Rand, Ayn. "Morality." *Ayn Rand Lexicon.*

Rawls, J. 1974. "The Independence of Moral Theory." Proceedings and Addresses of the *American Philosophical Association*, 48: 5–22.

Rhodes, Christopher. "Charlie Kirk and the Danger of Selective Empathy." Al Jazeera, 12 Sept. 2025, www.aljazeera.com/opinions/2025/9/12/charlie-kirk-and-the-danger-of-selective-empathy.

Richardson, K. (2004). IQ and the wealth of nations. Heredity, 92, 359–360. https://doi.org/10.1038/sj.hdy.6800418

Rindermann, H. (2012). Intellectual classes, technological progress, and economic development: The rise of cognitive capitalism. Personality and Individual Differences, 53(2), 108–113. https://doi.org/10.1016/j.paid.2011.07.001

Robins-Early, Nick. "AI's 'Oppenheimer Moment': Autonomous Weapons Enter the Battlefield." *The Guardian*, 15 Nov. 2024, www.theguardian.com/technology/article/2024/jul/14/ais-oppenheimer-moment-autonomous-weapons-enter-the-battlefield.

Robbins, K. (2022, December 26). Capitalism kills nearly 1 million Americans per year. Invisible People. Retrieved from https://invisiblepeople.tv/capitalism-kills-nearly-1-million-americans-per-year/

Rossom, Rebecca C et al. "Suicidal ideation reported on the PHQ9 and risk of suicidal behavior across age groups." Journal of Affective Disorders vol. 215 (2017): 77-84. doi:10.1016/j.jad.2017.03.037

Saed. (2021). Anti-communism and the hundreds of millions of victims of capitalism. Capitalism Nature Socialism, 32(1), 1–17. https://doi.org/10.1080/10455752.2021.1875603

Salahodjaev, R., & Kanazawa, S. (2017). Why do societies with higher average cognitive ability have lower income inequality? The role of redistributive policies. Journal of Biosocial Science, 49(4), 408–420. https://doi.org/10.1017/s0021932017000268

Scenic America. (2014). Billboard fact sheet. Retrieved from https://www.scenic.org/wp-content/uploads/2019/09/scenic20america20billboard20fact20sheet1.pdf

Scheper, Graham A. M. Ofer Hronrade-Defining the Long-Enigmatic "Hron" of Old English.

Schmitt, B., Brakus, J. J., & Biraglia, A. (2022). Consumption ideology. Journal of Consumer Research, 49(1), 74–95. https://doi.org/10.1093/jcr/ucab044

Schwitzgebel, Eric, et al. "Creating a Large Language Model of a Philosopher." Mind & Language, vol. 39, no. 2, July 2023, pp. 237–59.

Second Thought. "The AI Manhattan Project." *YouTube*, 10 Oct. 2025, www.youtube.com/watch?v=77oSBNvfpr4.

Shakespeare, W. (1992). *A Midsummer Night's Dream*. Mineola, NY: Dover Publications.

Singer, Peter. "Famine, Affluence, and Morality." *Philosophy and Public Affairs*, vol. 1–1, no. 3, season-01 1972, pp. 229–43. terpconnect.umd.edu/~dcrocker/Courses/Docs/Singer-Famine%20Affluence%20Morality.pdf.

Snedeger, Jean. "Flower power wilts." BBC News. Dec. 29, 1999. (Aug. 26, 2011) http://news.bbc.co.uk/2/hi/americas/575071.stm

Solow, R. M. (2003). Dumb and dumber in macroeconomics. Retrieved from https://fgeerolf.com/econ221/biblio/Solow2003.pdf

Stakelum, James Lee. "The End of AI Hallucinations: A Big Breakthrough in

Accuracy for AI Application Developers." Medium, 3 Sept. 2024, https://medium.com/@JamesStakelum/the-end-of-ai-hallucinations-a-breakthrough-in-accuracy-for-data-engineers-e67be5cc742a.

Stivers, M. (2021, June 30). How capitalism undermines progressive education reform. Jacobin. Retrieved from https://jacobin.com/2021/06/schooling-in-capitalist-america-progressive-education-reform

Sustainable Cooperative for Organic Development. (2019, October 11). Capitalism vs communism death tolls. Retrieved from https://scodpub.wordpress.com/2019/10/11/capitalism-vs-communism-death-tolls/

Tarnoff, Ben. "Weizenbaum's Nightmares: How the Inventor of the First Chatbot Turned Against AI." *The Guardian*, 1 Sept. 2023, www.theguardian.com/technology/2023/jul/25/joseph-weizenbaum-inventor-eliza-chatbot-turned-against-artificial-intelligence-ai.

The Editors of Encyclopaedia Britannica. "Satyagraha | Gandhi's Nonviolent Resistance, Civil Disobedience." Encyclopedia Britannica, 20 July 1998, www.britannica.com/topic/satyagraha-philosophy.

The Humanist Report. "Thoughts on Charlie Kirk, Empathy, and the Right's Double Standard for Political Violence." YouTube, 12 Sept. 2025, www.youtube.com/watch?v=3azViwC_dOA.

Themis, Stephan. "DrFeder.com — the Unassisted Birth Story of: Jessica Lynnae." *2008 Lauren Feder, M.D.*, 9 June 2008, drfeder.com/index.php?page=articles&action=viewArticle&articleID=7.

Thompson, Hunter S. "The Wave Speech – Fear and Loathing in Las Vegas." East Portland Blog, www.eastportlandblog.com/2012/07/23/the-wave-speech-fear-and-loathing-in-las-vegas.

Tinel, B. (2011). The Crisis of Neoliberalism. World Review of Political Economy, 2(1), 117–133.

Vanden Bosch, L. (2024, January 27). Success in capitalism requires the right kind of stupidity. Coping with Capitalism.

Van Der Werf, D. L. 2025. "The Shrinking Circle: Moral-Singularity and the Rise of Nativism." *Damiaan Luc van der Werf.*

Vernon, Anthony David. "BURN THE FLAG and PAINT THE CROSSWALKS." Daily Kos, www.dailykos.com/stories/2025/8/27/2340401/-BURN-THE-FLAG-PAINT-THE-CROSSWALKS.

Vernon, Anthony David. "Charlie Kirk Was an a**Hole." Medium, 24 Sept. 2025, medium.com/bouncin-and-behavin-blogs/charlie-kirk-was-an-a-hole-ceb928d4d0d9.

Vernon, Anthony David. "AI Can't Do Social Philosophy." *Medium*, HumanAI, 16 Oct. 2025, medium.com/p/edb6f58d63c9.

Vernon, Anthony David, and HstSethi. "Sophistry With Software." *Medium*, 19 Dec. 2024, medium.com/@antmanvernon305/sophistry-with-software-98a85ecd11b0.

Vernon, Anthony David. "Petty Disobedience." *Medium*, 30 Sept. 2025, medium.com/bouncin-and-behavin-blogs/petty-disobedience-386ffe29f078.

Vernon, Anthony David. "Philosophy With Robots." *Medium*, Philosophy Today, 26 Nov. 2024, medium.com/philosophytoday/philosophy-with-robots-8f5861ac5e68.

Vernon, Anthony David. ""Protest Against 287 (G) in the City of Miami." Miami-Dade Social Democrats, 17 June 2025, acidsocialdemocrats.substack.com/p/protest-against-287-g-in-the-city."

Vernon, Anthony David. "The Law Is Always Violent and Preference Driven." Medium, 3 July 2025, medium.com/philosophytoday/the-law-is-always-violent-preference-driven-d10ee4eea268.

Vernon, Anthony David. "Tyrants and the Death Penalty." Medium, 17 Sept. 2025, medium.com/activated-thinker/tyrants-the-death-penalty-ba4f1147cd61.

Vernon, Anthony David. "What Happened to Flower Power?" *Daily Kos*, www.dailykos.com/stories/2025/9/12/2343081/-What-Happened-To-Flower-Power.

Vold, Karina. ChatGPT: Rebel Without a Cause in "Philosophers on Next-Generation Large Language Models." *Daily Nous*, 16 Mar. 2023.

Waldrop, L. (2022, March 9). Commentary: GOP 'Socialists 'Propaganda Campaign Lacks Credibility. Tennessee Lookout.

Yadegaran, Jessica. "Extreme Home-birthing, Alone and Unassisted." *The Mercury News*, 28 Jan. 2014, www.mercurynews.com/2014/01/28/extreme-home-birthing-alone-and-unassisted-2/#:~:text=Navarre%20is%20trained%20as%20a,Cameron/Bay%20Area%20News%20Group).

Yastremsky, Michelle. The History of Flower Power | Petal Talk. www.1800flowers.com/articles/flower-facts/history-of-flower-power.

www.ingramcontent.com/pod-product-compliance
Lightning Source LLC
Chambersburg PA
CBHW071851230426
43671CB00012B/2146